To: Brownie & Rick, John, Tyler, Nicholas

Please know you are all the Best Care Givers in Brownie's world. Will be waiting for you at the end of the Rainbow Bridge

Chuicih

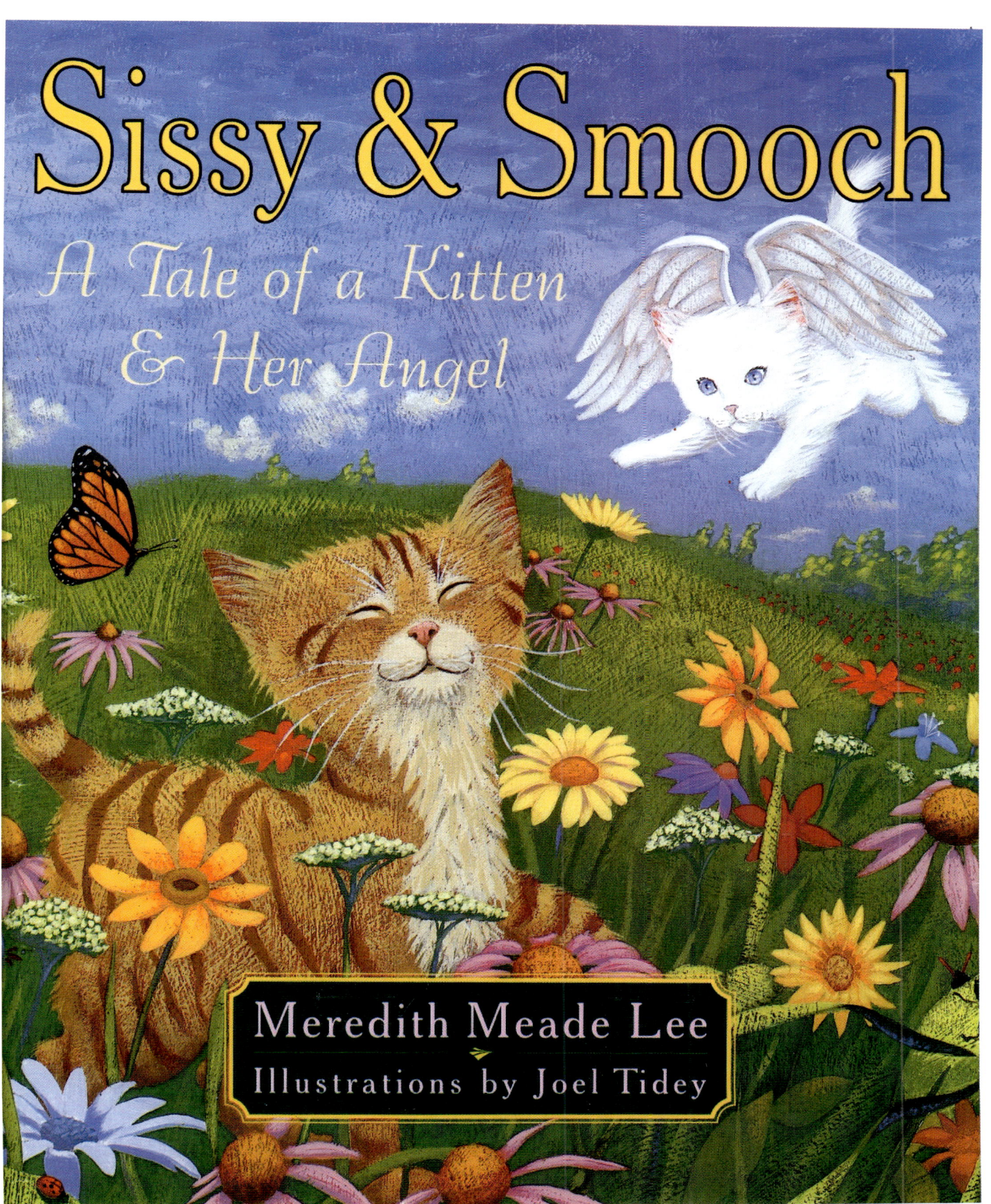

Sissy & Smooch™
"A Tale of a Kitten and Her Angel"©
BOOK & PLUSH SET

AUTHOR'S INTRODUCTION

Sissy & Smooch™, "A Tale of a Kitten and Her Angel"© is the first book of a four book Angel Series. As an author I feel responsible to give a sense of hope and encouragement to the children in our lives and in the lives of others. At a time when so many situations regarding children seems so fraught with conflict and violence I want my books to offer children an alternative to lashing outside of themselves and the opportunity to go inward with the spirit of their Guardian Angel. The gentle messages in my books teach the most simple lessons life has to offer, love, kindness, gentleness and most of all respect for oneself and for others. These messages are sent through kittens, puppies, little bugs and elegant eagles. Whether it be a child, animal or an adult, we are all here together to share love for one another and to assist each other on the extraordinary journey we call life.

Thank you. Meredith Meade Lee

PRODUCT INFORMATION

DESCRIPTION: "Sissy & Smooch, A Tale of a Kitten and Her Angel"© is a full size children's book with dust cover and set of two full size plush kittens. Sissy™ is a striped Earth Kitten, Smooch^{SM} is a White Guardian Angel Kitten.
Age Range: Two years and up
Book and Plush Toys come as a set in a fully illustrated collectable box.
Cost: $21.00

MARKETING INFORMATION

RETAIL:

Sissy & Smooch™ Book and Toys can be marketed to all of the retail book distributors as well as toy stores, gift shops and any other vehicle for retail sales.

ANIMATION:

"Sissy & Smooch"™ can be animated in a number of different ways. The Adventures of Sissy & Smooch as a children's cartoon series or in a feature film venue of "The Adventure of Sissy & Smooch." Written treatments for both of these options are available upon request.

MERCHANDISING:

"Sissy & Smooch"™ can be made smaller for merchandising for a feature film promotion. Given away or sold with a purchase from any of the popular franchised restaurants.

TELE-MARKETING:

"Sissy & Smooch"™ the book and plush set will make its tele-marketing debut on the QVC Shopping Network in September of 2000. This will give any retailer tremendous exposure for the product to aid in their personal marketing strategy.

ENTERTAINMENT AND PUBLIC RELATIONS:

AUTHOR: Meredith Meade Lee
TRADEMARK: Angel Michella^{SM}

ANGEL MICHELLA^{SM}: Meredith Meade Lee is Angel Michella^{SM}. Angel Michella^{SM} will be available to do any type of public relations with regard to her book and toys, including television, print, book signings, merchandising and any other form of marketing.
Author is an actress with 30 years experience in film and television.
Currently contracted with the QVC Shopping Network.

For Additional Information or to Order:
MEREDITH INTERNATIONAL LLC
CONTINENTAL ROAD
TUXEDO PARK, NY 10987
PH: 1-800-697-6111   INTERNATIONAL PH: (845) 351-3490   FAX: (845) 351-2624
www.sissyandsmooch.com

COPYRIGHT© 2000 MEREDITH INTERNATIONAL LLC

Sissy & Smooch

A Tale of a Kitten and Her Angel

Brownie ♡

Meredith Meade Lee

Illustrations • Joel Tidey

Text copyright © 1996 by Meredith Meade Lee

Illustrations copyright © 2000 by Joel Tidey

All rights reserved. No portion of this book may be reproduced—mechanically, electronically, or by any other means, including photocopying—without written permission of the publisher.

The Cataloging-in-Publication Data for this title is available from the Library of Congress.

ISBN 0-7611-2142-0

Produced by:

Workman Publishing Company
Custom Publishing Division
708 Broadway
New York, NY 10003-9555

First printing June 2000

Manufactured in China

First and foremost, I dedicate this book to God. Without His calling these books would never have come to pass. I will be forever grateful for His divine guidance and inspiration in these creations.

The angel series came to me within two weeks and the magical Christmas Classic within a year. I am honored to present you with the first of His gifts to me, and in turn my gift to our precious children.

Second, my deep appreciation to my loving husband, Charles Pierre. I could never have done this project without you. You are my love and my best friend.

Last, to the children, animals, and angels in our world. You are the special gifts from God, and we are all truly blessed to have you.

With all of God's love and light,

Judith Piyade Lee

Special Thanks from the Author

Creation is a gift from God. So are the special people that support the dreams of an author or artist. I express my sincerest appreciation to Workman Publishing and all of their talented creators. Special Projects Director Jenny Mandel for being the driving force behind this magical journey. Kate Tyler for seeing to the important details. Art Director Paul Gamarello for his professional guidance. Morris Taub for lending his creative gifts to this wonderful project. Production Director Wayne Kirn for moving the project forward and Jeff Bialosky from Treasures for being the captain of my creation, providing me with all of the valuable pieces to bring this magic to fruition. You are all Angels in my world.

Once upon a time in a magical land, there lived a King and Queen of Cats. The King and Queen of Cats were so very special, for you see, they were Angels. They had beautiful shimmering wings and golden halo crowns. The King and Queen of Cats had very important duties in their Angel Kingdom. It was their duty to insure that each cat that lives on Mother Earth has its very own Guardian Angel.

Now, you wonder, what is a Guardian Angel? A Guardian Angel is a friend or guardian that watches over each creature. A Guardian Angel Cat is with each individual cat to love and protect it the best they can. Guardian Angels are our friends in all circumstances. In times of joy as well as troubled times.

On this particular day, the King and Queen of Cat Angels were quite upset. It appears a kitten down on Mother Earth was not given a Guardian Angel. Now the kitten was alone and in quite a bit of trouble.

The King and Queen immediately used their magical Angel powers to create a Guardian Angel for this tiny kitten.

The King bellowed, "There will be no mistakes in my kingdom. This little kitten must have a Guardian immediately."

The Queen pointed her paws to the heavens. Lightning bolted and thunder clapped. The clouds twirled all around and threw sparks throughout the heavens.

Before all the Angels' eyes, out rolled a fluffy, silvery white kitten with stardust eyes.

The King and Queen were pleased. They named their newest Angel Smooch. "Go, Smooch," said the King and Queen, "down to Mother Earth to protect the lost little kitten."

Little gossamer wings sprouted from Smooch's back. "I can fly now," Smooch beamed. Smooch could feel her Angel spirit beating with such great joy.

Smooch took a big practice loop into the heavens and now, sure of her wings, she dove towards earth. All of the Angel Cats sang a chorus of praise.

Down on Planet Earth, Sissy felt very alone in her tiny cage in the small animal shelter. Sissy tried to remember where her mother and all her brothers and sisters were. She soon drifted into a deep sleep. As she slept, a dream came to her. Sissy saw herself playing in a field with a friend, but her friend could fly!

A kitten with wings, Sissy thought in her dream. "My name is Smooch," said the little Angel. "Hello, Smooch, my name is Sissy. Why do you have wings?" "Because I am your Guardian Angel. I am here to love and protect you whenever I can." "Well, I certainly need you now!" In her dream, Sissy began to wish and pray for her Angel Smooch to come and help her.